TOTALITY

By the same author:

Aril Wire (2018)

TOTALITY

ANDERS VILLANI

RECENT
WORK
PRESS

Totality
Recent Work Press
Canberra, Australia

Copyright © Anders Villani, 2022

ISBN: 9780645356359 (paperback)

 A catalogue record for this
book is available from the
National Library of Australia

Cover image: *Celestial Dog* © Tyler Arnold, 2022
Internal images: © Tyler Arnold, 2022
Cover design: Recent Work Press
Set by Recent Work Press

recentworkpress.com

For Emily

Contents

MORAVIAN ECLIPSE MYTH

THIRD CONTACT

FOURTH CONTACT

The shadow always has a shape, the shape of the body which carries it.

—Francis Ponge, 'The Sun Placed in the Abyss,'
translated by Serge Gavronsky

To the All-Powerful

Climb the bunk ladder and make me selfish.
How many birch sprigs should I gather?

Climb the bunk ladder and make me selfish.
How many cypress sprigs should I gather?

Make me selfish. Grant me a founding.
How many birch sprigs should I gather?

The millipede wishes to wake a spiral.
How many cypress sprigs should I gather?

Grant the millipede cause. Make me selfish.
How much birch sprigs should I gather?

The millipede wishes for Saturn to smell it.
How many cypress sprigs should I gather?

For Saturn to love it and Saturn to recoil from it.
How many birch sprigs should I gather?

Climb the bunk ladder and make me selfish.
How many cypress sprigs should I gather?

Climb the bunk ladder and make me selfish.
How many birch sprigs should I gather?

FIRST CONTACT

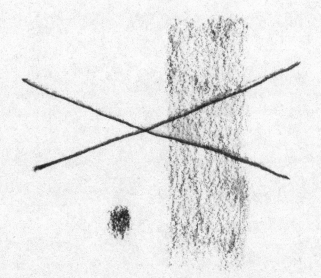

Alabaster

Somewhere between spirit
and appetite, a boy
untangles teabag strings, lifts
floor dust with wet hands.

Redbacks observe him
from the cornices, and boys.
Any hotter, and he'd have woken in hospital
on IV, not here. Not alone.

Sweat pearls the salt lamp in the den.
Alabaster men grapple
atop the piano—white-
eyed, posed and white-lipped.

He knows well not to do this.
Not to walk to the church
op shop, root for knives whose
cheap handle rivets whirl

on the tang. Whose slabs
peel. Not to pull from the bargain bin
a bag of pressed flowers, secret
petals beneath the knife handles,

seal them with superglue,
a found tube. Not to be wasps in the grass
or minigolf holes or hoses.
Not to blindfold. Not to touch, not

to tell, not to read, not to let the sun
shudder him, squeal him
like not a boy. His cinnamon sticks,
his juice bottles. His yellow

assembly place. His forty-plus, his
park, his yabby pond, his voice
in drowned bark missives, his bed
-eaten ankles.

Latencies

You showed me after dinner.
        Those pills on your marl trackpants

as you led me up to your room, the sum
        hazing, like gas. I was seventeen and

stainless. Laundry dunes near
        racks assembled on the boxes, wine

-scabbed shag, teethed headboard.
        Milk coffees in stoneware mugs—

desk, dresser, beside table—top-dressed
        with mould. You led, levelled, hid.

Through muslin, maimed comb,
        Melbourne skyline, shards of verse from

your epics: boys my brother knew
        had done spells in Lara. Boys I'd kill

to carry, voice, surrogate. Those baby
        portraits shrining the walls. Your

mum at her easel, anxious to paint
        over the cowed accomplice to this.

Once, a girl at school called me *clean*.
        Did I wash in spares? Was my soap Dove?

Olive? Lead the way to having heard it.
        Scar tissue's paraffin, candelabra, taste of

moon solder, bike shorts you wore
at the river. Lycra square as a frame.

For M

Interferer

io nel pensier mi fingo; ove per poco
il cor non si spaura.
—Giacomo Leopardi, 'L'infinito'

Above the cane fields, whispering
kites figure-eight, quieting
harvester engines their signal

to swoop for carrion. Blade-ground
mice. Taipans. Through the car window
he draws a circle around each bird,

chains it, until its wings solve riddles
his ankles tense and untense.
No answer, and the bird starves.

He cries to think of starving it.
Of having no choice. It's the same
when the rainbow Las Vegas

in his head when the lights die
must all beam yellow that instant
if the possum in their guttering isn't to burst

into cabbage moths. Or his promise
of tops and tails of *fagiolini*,
dingo claws, to the sun—when it's not close

to enough to forgive what his nipples
accuse his thumbs of. Or when Dad
won't wake for third cuddles, and has to drown.

Zio Renato ate snake in the 50's. Mythic snake-
stock *brodo*. Fat, macheted
air sopping with cutters' Italian, dialect.

A man chases him home from Luke's.
The man's machete sour with rust and burnt cane.
The man knows.

Or at Coles, when a new song starts, and a voice
whispers the pack with the almond
—lift his tongue, shelter.

Log Entry

rest stop b/w thunder
bay / winnipeg / lost
root-beer virginity / blowjob
from gaspésie—unnamed
or named origin—in road
-house toilet stall / gave
gaspésie head for aeons
beforehand / baroquely
whorled / shoulder blades
in bowl / back of head
oiling cistern / whole saint
lawrence estuary in my ears
/ peninsula of whales /
surplus light / no breath
through nobody's lungs
/ gaspésie finished / i
flashed hooks of recurrence /
next Tim Hortons next
temple of pink liquid soap /
morose, baitless hooks /
on road again / skimming
book on ocean freight /
spotifying debussy / nsync
 / streaming micro-plastic
polemics / dreaming of unboiled
lake water in my mouth /
dreaming of lake sturgeon / dreaming
of lake waves down my throat
as i surf them / am i melbourne
or third-body bath / root
-beer cup rim mauled to
styrofoam confetti / a wedding /

spit confetti into seat pocket
across aisle / gaspésie asleep /
basswood / grace note /
nameless bloom / asleep / bridal /
bride of erasure's prairies

Pedagogy

　　　　　You don't teach the child to chainsaw
but that red box is full
　　　　　of snow. You don't teach them to bite
the ore nugget under
　　　　　Nonna's mattress, but that the Pilbara
gets kissed at bedtime
　　　　　because stars too vie for Jesus. You
don't teach them
　　　　　where the neighbour's beard sparks,
where t-bone fat braids

　　　　　into the neighbour's singlet threads
but how to lock-pick
　　　　　the garage with all the broken-down
soft-serve machines.
　　　　　You don't teach them mouth, aperture,
sputter, curdle, but leopard
　　　　　cub and teat. You don't teach balloons
glued to PVC pipe ends.
　　　　　They don't need to be retaught. You
don't teach them rock
　　　　　opens to dirt when it finds a nape

but that linseed oil
　　　　　oozes free, and mandarins do cry tonight.
You don't teach them
　　　　　ice floes patrol hot baths, flushed skin, but
point to the mast
　　　　　and fling them nails. You don't teach
them to dissolve
　　　　　a tin of Danish shortbread in chain oil.
They're the same nails.
　　　　　You don't teach them to love a body

to vanishing, but that
　　　　doesn't mean you don't. At some level
you know this. You don't
　　　　teach them tender reprieve's chenille
is doused in ethanol and
　　　　already combusting, but that sick to miss
what they miss, they
　　　　risk forgetting the guard. You don't teach
them to matador a rusted
　　　　lawn edger, but that circles cut straightest.

Fight Night Massage

He samples a little Egyptian almond oil
in the aisle before they buy it, sweet as blackstrap, the grocery
radio blares the undercard and her lemon juice concentrate's
label is in Arabic too wonderful to focus on, she downs the whole bottle
at the register to halt her period for the night
she tells him, *hold Demeter at bay*, within
seismic earshot of the grocer who fumbles the persimmons
in his hands that sour-bent she points to, stuffs in her
anorak pocket where her phone pings
like eucalyptus leaves
surrendering bushfire their oil
that could be more matches, more filtered ab offerings, more ice
-breaking Tinder quips, billboards across town plug it,
they hit the rum on each of the six flights of stairs, strobing
blood raves by the top, is the plastic beneath the sateen
Airbnb linens ultrasound gel, go splash

around in it, she has him put her stomach in it
as if she were getting an ultrasound, and it's no mere title
bout but unification, every belt on the line, the Good
Lord at rest is restive pained is morphine, and because he doesn't
know her it's cool to oil his cupped left hand and fire
-stick it hot, short the earpiece, watch flexion gnarl
his lips friction spatter the dankness
while vertebrae
glint like studs, coccyx sweat-berried, poets
smell the ink of the universal book like a sweet fat on night's ribs, he chants
the Italian word for persimmon, *cacho, cacho*, a glaze on night's ribs,
they eat some, tonsils
moss, she licks blackstrap off the sheets, which are red, who the fuck
buys red sheets, but this is no bedroom, it's a doctor's surgery, it's an ore
vein, it's the symbol two strangers' mouths form, unfenced mouths, and the rum
kicks in, but not the lemon juice, skin of hot fruit, event of hot valley
terraformed by wolves, pore, den.

Terms

She drives from Detroit to meet him.
    At the arboretum two green snakes
        cross the path and become the Huron.

They subdivide the passive. He gets
    the lion's share, by not asking.
        Her accent gets more Long Island.

Deer crack a cipher of border
    fence holes, ravenous for flowering
        weeds they must poison this side.

Churches want her sex store gone.
    Can you gentle a deer like a foal?
        Can I hit you? Tonight has to be calculated.

Kites, unpanicked in warm grass.
    Cottonwood seed, riding fairground
        pirate ships above the Huron.

Two green snakes. Two clitorises
    on his chest—he regrets how this
        torch siphons air, regrets how history

ups the voltage in its fences around
    the carnal. Yes, hit me. Already
        calculations have crowbarred his

apartment window open, leapt—specular
    lust for help a deer
        of white-hot flowers. She's the one

he'll dare ketamine with in private
        back rooms of every after-party
                in every Detroit while every arthouse

porn film beams onto every wall.
        For him, she'll ghost every city.
            Two green snakes cross the path
            and become the Huron.

Intervals

The garage door lowers.
There is no afternoon.
I beam the halogens, lock

the door to the house,
consider barring it. Ease
the bike incline to level.

Admit to three things
ahead of me. One: volcano
panograph on the wall

pitching like a soft master
over cobalt ocean somewhere
in the South Pacific.

Two: full-length mirror,
frame painted cobalt
with paint unfit for purpose

—globs, runnels. My
shirtless body in the mirror, sweat
-ripe navel hair an estuary.

Three: slabs of golden
doghair and pinkish lint
on top of the drier.

Intervals of thrash and limpness,
of volcano and you leading
me from the lecture theatre,

of a powerful thirty-year-old man's
torso and doghair. Admit my
pumped arms cross my body in an X

I laugh at, spill limp for.
The spokes blur. The spokes
still to panorama.

Smoke Alarm

A couple rents a pool house for the weekend in their own city.
Bathrobes, scent diffusers (plug-outlet and bamboo), bed lamps
seized by voice, mini-fridge Riesling. Burgundy lace garter, shutout
blinds. Brochures on a side table. They role-play, with accents. Her
Russian reminds him of his dad, who did a Cossack dance once,
body of the underpants frayed from the waistband like buttery
shank from the bone. It's so the wax takes, he tells her when he sticks
his boots in the oven. It opens the pores. While she rubs her scars
with silicone gel and gets her new bikini top right, he visits the garage.
Guests don't have access. Twice noise drops him in a cupboard
under the workbench that smells of wood stain, shards of stiff
expanding foam fused toothlike to the door. When it's real quiet
he licks salt, sand, off boogie-board fiberglass. Half drags some lie lows
off a shelf. The spa is heated to forty-one like her favourite pool at
the hot springs, and her hand drips the skyline from it. There's a
brochure for the hot springs—nothing on the person caught with
cygnets slaughtered by the billabong; nothing about how one night
in the hilltop pool, a ringtail possum neared the edge to drink, she
seized his arm, and he recoiled, apologised, praised the ringtail.

Ansett

An attendant points to the boy.
Would he like to see the flight deck?

He fills his pockets with Lego, every
thigh prick a shot of daring.

On his bare feet, the aisle carpet
feels as he imagined

the red carpet in the basilica on TV
at Nonna's felt to the bishops,

barefoot under their *paramenti*. Footsteps
—his, Mum's, and the attendant's, her

hair a carved hunk of obsidian—
drown in the engine surf. A toilet

flush sucks something from him.
Before he can say what it is, he sees

as he's imagined seeing—through
the nose. Less sky than star. All the nickel

blind chains he burst because
they were rosaries and raked across

Nonna's black soil to unsalt it.
He sees the captain folding the hands

of another boy, whom he hates,
into strong hands and the yoke.

Vintage

first a white room
then plums

next door the old woman boots a recycling tub through her jungle
rattles every snail removes
her dew-dark uggs

winemaker
     don't you hear

from the bridgehead
a general orders his companies

to vintage themselves

first threatless
then plums

you put your suitcase and oil heater in the boot and I grab purplish
clumps of Great Dane fur

(the last owner a breeder)

matted into the ceiling
rake them over a lamp post

don't you hear
     first a white room

then plums
then the order

Doctrine

Peals for his daily
provident walk /
science building to bike
shed / up the social
rungs to the back oval
(maybe labile cool
kids call out after him /
plain-clothed detectives
at his headphones'
door) / where hot frost
-melt darkens the Calvin
Klein cuffs his brother
said to roll / along the
meat of the oval fence /
thumbing road dust off
the chain link / dust
from the unpaved road
between school and the farm
that grows *hand-grenades* /
artichokes the cool kids keep
caches of beneath their
kiff-smeared benches /
towards the black
beetle colonies (a species
he made in grade two tunnel
down his ear canal so nurse
would hold his head
while the syringe flushed)
charcoaling tennis court
baselines / synthetic grass
sand he sometimes tastes
that tastes of his crèche
sand / vinyl sleep mats /

fennel gating the padlocked
dress-ups shed / hygienist's
bubblegum toothpaste
the day they learnt to brush
foaming at the corners of
pretty Natalie's pinker-
than-the-tooth-paste lips as she
looked at him / just him /
and smiled a trust smile /
around the gymnasium
/ here loneliness
chemicals war like salt
in an estuary for influence
but upstream, against flight /
against the buoyancy of sinking
—warm, fathomless—into
himself / past the prettiest girls
whose contests judge him
the prettiest boy / in words
that scrim the sun / who
don't know his lips
last night made trembling
contact with his penis
which was not his penis
which was a memory
which was a carpet of *nespola* pits
which was a banquet table
which was plum vinegar
which was a caulking gun
which was a hieroglyph
which was a spit brother
which was a compressed spring
which was glass and black sand
which was the Discman's AA's
which was a virus
in the cells of a virus

in the marrow of solitude
barred to solitude
while the cistern refilled /
who call him up
himself because he won't
do / show he lives to do /
what a pretty boy's on earth
to do with pretty girls
according to the pealing
lunch-bell doctrine / whom
he lets eclipse him with hate /
lust's liver free to soften
providently in its milk /
past the leisure-centre
-chlorine paperbarks / through the
staff-only lot / back to
the mix's dreamy opener

Face of Glory

there's a   moral
obligation   here

i wish   there
weren't

but   you   must
be risk   aversive

and   by law
transparent

until your blood
work   returns

you must   assume
you are   reactive

SECOND CONTACT

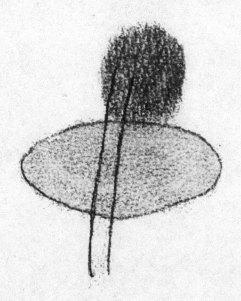

Mural

Somewhere between harsh surf
and instinct, the boy plays a game.
The objective—murder
each wave, each lunging enemy.

Handfuls of sand are mines
he springs on crests, detonates.

Bellies of red tablets swell across the house
as if laid by a sleepwalker, all sweet
coatings sucked off.

At school, the boy greets his friends
down by the rebound wall, with its rainbow
-and-dolphin mural.
They hurt each other here.

If his friends cry, or go easy, the boy shows them
how it's done. Because

his bomber has embroidered on the breast
his initials in red felt, the boy assigns
labels the power to reveal what is
under mastery, his to know in full.

In this way, the boy loses the blackness
hemming him when he's near flight.

The boy's recall of brand slogans, jingles,
product ingredients, clothing tags,
blurbs, verges on encyclopedic.

Every moment, every action, is furtive.
When someone is looking
but not, he eats scabs, boogers, eye sleep.

One day, a myna hits his window.
He weeps with the silver in his diaphragm.
Douses a redback, later, in Lynx Africa.
Lights it, and it's birdsong.

Harvest

The figs have come in.   You open your eyes.
It's day.   Some canvas flaps in ribbons.
You'll need a ladder.   You aren't dreaming.
No livestock dead in the dam.   Vines spool
around gas pipes on the roof the upper

> -most figs canopy.   It's day.   Milk in a bowl
> aids your sleep.   You aren't dreaming.   Motorbike
> song.   Everyone wears white linen on ladders.

The sky fat with sugar gliders.   Light
rips the canvas more.   The figs have come in.
You open your eyes.   No test results true
none unburned.   You aren't dreaming.   It's a real
hole in the heart. Wing gusts urge your father's

> face: harshen against revelation.   Ripeness scent.
> Don't step to the danger rung with sparkling feet.
> Reach. Hyperextend your shoulders.

You're a millionaire in a blimp full of coins.
You're a Gatling gun.   You're not memory.
You stand how angels on trees stand.   It's day.   Harvest.
You aren't dreaming.   You open your eyes.
Ladders remind you of your father.
It's day.   You utter your first words as they

> were recorded on the white of a photograph.
> *Ladder.   Aerial.*
> The figs leak milk into a bowl.   It's day.

Gravel Dump, Northern Victoria

On your lips, cold butane
-canister sweat. You pour

the billycan of oolong
over my head and pigment
wraiths come to laugh with us. In a woodpile

near our tent, an animal decomposes.
While we bet on the species, a family
in silhouette plays blackjack.

You say hawk. I say mouse. We both sense I'm right
on the brink of repulsion
at my own lust, of not touching you
except with resentment. What are our options?

Liniment each other's calves, snap
gravel blades and inhale
this seed quiet. Have you buried

a dead thing / is it appropriate
to fuck so near a family
walled off by nylon tissue /

Remember when the semi spilled its load
of offal across the Hume, we gagged,
you said get help or you were done, and we were detoured
up a dirt track, past a bluestone church?

Tomorrow, the molasses
mill tour. Sorghum farming. If the farm
shop sells oilskins, or boiled
wool blankets, I'll hang back, cut surgeon's masks.

Contingencies. A ringtail possum
in your driveway that didn't look hurt
but whose front teeth were
dipped in sap / what looked like sap /

Could it have been molasses /
could you wear my neck to sleep /

Gunnamatta

They drove to the Rye landfill,
he and his father. The yard waste
they'd loaded overtopped the hired
trailer's cage, disabling the rear view.

At the gate, a pigtailed attendant
directed them, like air traffic, to
the correct pit for organic materials.
Next to the pit were house-sized

mulchers set to graded finenesses, steam
firming above the heaps like clouds
above the Dandenongs. The trailer
reached the pit edge.

His father threw powerfully, shoveled
with spring-loaded thrust. Promised
a trip to Gunnamatta to watch the surfers

once the trailer was emptied, he fidgeted
like the gulls in the gull-overcast
fidgeted with their bodies,
fat with fossicked food scraps, fording

the wind's currents to sea.
Another tree flew. He couldn't stay where he was.
Skipped to the junkyard store.
Where I can see you, Anders!

Pots and pans made from dud metals,
lounge settings hacked at with axes,
infomercial ab elixirs, towers of
bald car tyres. Against a shard mirror

leant someone's flower portraits
done with too much paint—his fingers
pruned petal from filament, sepal
from stem, clumps of vase from vase,
all flavourless and resplendent.

Gunnamatta's bravest, everyone knew,
paddled out near the pumping station
despite the sewer outflow.
There the swells were hugest.

That was where his father would take him.
That was what he could smell
when, in a big box whose fibreboard
had regressed to the scalloped layer,
the seabed layer, he found videos.

All over the covers, stars twinkled
on the naked bodies of ladies and men
posed like he'd been shown
who looked at him. Exultant, warlike.
The constellation's signs and sentinels.

On Truemans Road, he saw a roo
long after they'd passed its carcass now
the trailer was unloaded. Spacious
joy spooled out inside him. The roughs
and fairways of golf courses glistened

in cloud-break sunlight as the ocean
would be sparkling for it, if the sky didn't shutter.
They passed the thoroughbred agistment.
Paddocks gave over to tea tree scrub,

flatlands to dunes. Gunnamatta was salt
in the air, in his blood. It was expansion
and brightness. But, today, not water.
It was trailer-tyre marks on the moaning

shoulder, before the final ridge peaked.
A video cassette, flung powerfully into
tea-tree warrens, lost. The lukewarm
bonnet—thermostat unopened—
he was laid on while his father thought.

Ecstatic Fields

Remember this: your first taste of speed.
Scratch the white-out
graffiti tags off his stereo's tape decks
until you bleed beneath the nails. Let the iron
pica cleanse the palate and laugh a bit and be hard.

Five years ago, you sucked wet cement like cloth.
Now, you're on the back of a stolen 750cc
dirt bike hurtling through a playground.
That blaze up your calf? Your polyester-nylon
pant leg, melted by the muffler, skin's next resin.

You've doctored the aniseed. The day you suffer
your last winter lay-by from Target
it's spitting. The spit smells of Red Rooster salt.
No carpark spaces, except in the open air.
You bolt your mother's Ford Laser. The spit
burns up on your eyelids. Far behind, your mother
hums, unaware she hums. A dirge she often
hides in cat lyrics, like sweetbreads in risotto.

Five of you Uber to Brunswick at an hour when the light's
unaware it's light. Your driver trades crypto; at reds
and through greens he sings to an infant
altcoin. You can't make him name it. Not this early. Copper
and verdigris. Bear and bull. As you spill out, he blesses your futures.

Mr. Whipped, the NOS deliveryman,
has backorders. Waiting, you play ping pong,
heat cocktail spring rolls to abandon, steal your host's
housemate's shiraz gin and Sicilian olives, empty
baggies onto a cheese board and mix
dye pigments. Over the techno, over the hiss

someone presses you about your first time
eating black liquorice, the loneliest
question. A cat scratches its ottoman—
what's left of it. Language and hydrogen fuse.
Ingrowns split like atoms. You're ready.

Intervals

Crossed hands say, *None*
but gods may enter. Worldly is the air
-lock that seals

this chamber. Return, return.
There is no afternoon.
I raise the incline not much

past the hill at my primary school
where I and another blonde
white kid are photographed

for a new glossy brochure
like the faculty one you ask me
in your office to pose for. Intervals

of pearly whites, of baby-wiping
en tout cas off tennis-racquet frame
pre-shoot, of doghair, of lint

and volcano.
Aum tattoo on my trapezius.
Aum in my throat molasses

gaslighting itself to honey.
Was there a skylight in your office
tattooed with myna feet? The man

WD40-ing the cobalt door
to the room in which a blonde
white girl and I pose for the '01

junior-school brochures.
She and I kiss that evening. Bite
off each other's enamel. Of tongue

harpoons, of heartrate
kites. Of the son she has now—his Dora cup.
Of the boy who failed me.

Gravitron

He goes with his brother and his brother's friends to Luna Park.
When he kisses Nonna goodbye, she is on her Sunday couch topping
and tailing *fagiolini*, farting as she trembles. Mum has put *Miserere* on again,
band-aids over her eyebrows again. Boots (Nonna calls him *the grey*)
rumbles on the couch back, bites Nonna's hair, white as his paws, a little as
he washes it. Do he and his brother know Nonna's cousin sang with Maria Callas?
He's never travelled to the city without one of his parents. At Watsonia two men
maul each other. At Fairfield the big boys jump off, and back on at the last second.
They kick the tram open and race through the giant mouth, like in his dream.

The big boys' zippered shorts pockets bulge he doesn't know what with.
He buys a dagwood dog, a squeeze packet of sauce. He likes the batter
so much that part of him isn't biting it. His brother and his brother's friends
ride the Big Dipper while he sits in a thoroughfare, picking his nose.
A freckled girl he would fuck points and asks why are your legs pink. It's *en tout cas*
from a tennis court. You have to water them before and after each set.
She asks what a set is. He can't explain it. Yesterday morning, the white
hose kept kinking, he was too weak to unkink it, so one of the dads took over.
Next, they ride the Gravitron. It looks like the Millennium Falcon.
Riders form a ring, backs against the slanted, matted wall panels.
Lit like his bedroom ceiling, the Gravitron whirls, lifts everyone off the floor.
His brother and his brother's friends haul themselves upside down

and drive their reverse bodies into crazy shapes, hair like blowtorch tips.
He tries to match the big boys, like in his dream. The gravity's too strong—
he's pinned. From a pod in the centre the operator controls the speed, the music,
the lights. His brother and his brother's friends unzip their shorts pockets.
They take out fart bombs in silver pouches, squeeze them, and the Gravitron slows.
A voice says to evacuate. He and his brother and his brother's friends
do the dodgem cars. He gets blitzed. Security eyes them. They buy the big pretzels
with the big salt. He locks his crystals in his left hand for when it's just him.
His brother wins a cap gun in the laughing-mouth-and-ball game, loads it.

Diminution, Dream, Embellishment

A disco. Adults on one side
of the light-up dance floor, children on the other.
A child breakdances. A circle forms.

Nonna lies glum on the shag.
Her house: clammy with shit.

Scusa. Scusa. Ambulance.

My parents' desktop is signed in
to my brother's email address.
Better not log out. Better not look.

The LED tiles become sacs of scorpion venom.
The child head-spins, splits the sacs.
Every spattered face in the circle.

I picture Kimberley chancing upon me, shitting
in the stream of her hair's shadow.

No pity brings the streams. No pity
brings me to the brim
of the black hat Earth wears
when I dive into its pupil.

Blood after my blood, on the sofa
dismantling the last adult
photograph of yourself—who
writes you? On what business?

Bracketed to the wall, next to Christ: mandolin
built by ancestors on Elba, strings
gut, but which beast of burden?

One antivenin: the child's mother
must drop a dinner plate so softly it doesn't crack
and, picking up one pea at a time, dancing,
declare it wrong for her to have given birth.

Greenhouse Entrance Bell

identical
to the bell
on the lost–cat–
poster–smeared
door of the milk bar
where after school
he and big brother
would buy sour worms
five cents each
gobble them battery
tongued at the yabby pond
down the road where
years later he secreted
his first man's underpants
red as the Testarossa
he'd been gunning
did a ceremony of it
a whole delirious
liturgy the sky
black and cloud–plated
black snake its belly
blooming white fungus
waistband elastic
crimped like the roof
of a staghound's mouth
a staghound's black mouth
before it went him
like cicatrices not
supposed to yolk
over eyes like a wishing
coin into the fountain
at the plaza food court

where peace lily
leaves came of age
so big they could hide
a man's body a man's
wrongs he ringed
the legs over rush
shadows
rode

uphill with his wish bells

Marlin

A pupil appears at school early
to lick the flagpole and speak different.
Scratch the 'g' from 'listening'

like the girl he watches
hang her beaded bag
from the hook with all the grace he doesn't know

he heaps upon her.
At recess, the pupil eats a golden delicious,
seed and stem. Each instant a northswept

southerner in Nonna's stories, losing dialect.
Kids jigsaw around him; he stays still
faster than they do. The sun sinks

into its resin.
Seven bells. The girl he watches untense
her hand, as if she almost

imitates a marlin, but stops herself—
how does she stop herself? Why

does he see her at her bag
rubbing lanolin cream from a white jar
on the webbing between fingers that understand him now?

This shared language must be rung in.
At lunch, the pupil scrapes a beetle off a wattle bush

and fills his ear. Screeches
down the canal, barbed
legs pricking towards the drum.

B's Stepdad's

They're only boys
who used to frolic and play…
—Fadwa Tuquan, 'Song of Becoming,' translated by Naomi Shihab Nye

The house was a palace where kings ruled.
The house had a marble birdbath.
The house taught how to open your eyes with a girl.
A speedball dangled in the basement.
The house smelt of Lynx Africa and pie gravy.
The house's boots were steel-capped
—some smaller than a man's hand.
The house's elders taught the Word—*wog,*
curry-muncher, boong, slut, cocksucker, gimp, gook, retard.

The downstairs windows of the house flashed.
The house had a view of the King Lake ranges.
The house had quarter-ounces that came with a Cadbury Rose
of your choice. The house was a palace.
The house had a smoke machine—raspberry.
The house had whip racked on a *Ralph* calendar.
The house had Southern Cross flags.
Boys in fat pants shuffled to hardstyle in the patio
where the house should have had a back door.

A hangman's noose dangled in the basement.
The house taught how not to be a faggot
—how to mix records, how to launch an elbow.
You're a faggot if you read books, or don't smell this hand.
The house was a wonderland with no day and no night
and no king who hadn't rubbed the sawn-off for luck.
The house's bed-sheet curtains were lizards.
The house's leggings were carousel ponies.
Up and down, up and down, up and down.

The house's pit bulls flew at sirens.
The house had home-brand tomato sauce
with too much sugar in it, too little vinegar.
The house was a palace where kings ruled.
The front door of the house was battering-rammed.
Four pairs of the house's steel-capped boots
could have fit in the dangling hands.
The house's windows were newspapered.
The house became a birdbath.

Sunday Salesman

Anglican bells. Horns down the park
each wicket. Red Eye shimmies home
from Bundoora pub, levels a lamb's

ear by his letterbox, hymns the usual
Skyhooks medley on his belly
propping up flowers like Mum once

picked glass off her bedroom floor.
You're across the road with a rag
and old Redbacks, a tin of polish

too purple for the leather. Your 4 SALE
sign leans against the nature-strip
linden—a Coco Pops box panel.

Hours have rung. No one's stopped.
Close to no one's passed (your street's
not that near a main road). Night

watchman: clouds not that long off
the galah a warrior will ride to Olympus
to answer Mum's dinner pleas.

Next door, the Panelbeater buffs
the red Ford Escort in his driveway.
He's been doing it up forever.

Hours ago he said g'day and now
in trackies not much different to the buffing
rags he drifts across.

Any buyers? Any girls at school?
Root as many as you can, Ace. Remember that
when you're older.

The Panelbeater looks both ways,
helps Red Eye to his feet. You hear
the name *Allan* and the door opens.

Abacus

Wolf, Dragon, and Frog bait Kalparrin Lake's shadows for redfin
one summer. All summer they hook carp and eels. Haul the catch
ashore, sweet with mud the red lips drool.

Take note of the stain sound—carp smeared against cheek, dragon
-fly lips, iridescent nylon tracksuit. Take note of the day Wolf,
Dragon, and Frog eat the sun.

(Don't call them oracles. Don't flatten them. Call them *cacho* tongue
moss, or the sweet wind as Fantales unwrap.)

On this day, clear line spooled thick-blue as punishment, they drop
their rods, lay a gum branch over fence logs near a Falcon post
-crime-spree on the lakebed,

gurgling. Hack off centipede bark. Whittle tips to arrowheads. Rack
each carp's throat, each abacus bead. Take note of the anglers'
kitten—how their mother howls

when they storm the den, burnt-match-and-ammonia dusk, but not
the tabby, who near ends himself

for these non-redfin, these failures, hissing back rivals who might dare.
Who sits in the yard all night, all sundead day, vomiting. Calm. Malcontent even
to be dragged from the bones.

Befana

Epiphany Eve, late. Befana
brings him figs and *caramelle*.
It's forbidden to see her.
He does, but she doesn't
spear him with her broom handle.
She mops the kitchen lino,
buffs it, presses her lips to his
blonde crown, lights the furnace
of blessing. You're a ghost, boy.
You haven't met your wealth.
He studies his arms. To his cheeks
they're winter pillowcases
almost too terrible to lie on.
See. Haunt. See through. Opt
to be nothing. This is ghosthood.
None in the haunted world
enjoy such clearance. Will his
fig-seeded teeth help grant it?
Will his *caramelle* lips be gentle?
Will he advocate? Will he give
thanks? Even the leopard
cracks urine whips that corral
other leopards their territory.
He doesn't understand Befana.
This talk in Italian of advocating and leopards.
This talk of the black sugar,
the figs of garlic she'll bring
when he's grown. Figs of sawdust.
He doesn't word-know he's sick
to tell Befana he's been knifing
a prow through the hall and she should
sip some bilge from his hands.
That he spins. That every degree he spins
someone more colts outward.

Love and Withdrawal Postscript (as Preamble)

He'll approach you on a peak-hour train.
You'll be writing in a Nepalese notebook
and he'll stand over you and ask what.

You'll let yourself.
The Nullarbor will flood. Weeks will flood.
The sun will stand over the promontory.

Inlet a moon
of apple, mud-flat-peeled. Steaming, like your hot
mint scalp. Snapdragons. You'll have compared

montes pubis the night before. Called them anthills.
Wind will hammer dress to skin. He'll watch
immodesty flood you for the first time

since you looked up and covered the cursive
like a yawning mouth. You'll eat Saturn

peaches, fuck *in absentia*, your representative
careful not to taste the air or name him
or exploit him like you've realised he's taught,

urged, lovingly, the Nullarbor having woken
wrung into the Yarra, fingernails having begun to whisper

    it isn't right what you're doing.

Echidnas will raid the deck compost.
You'll mince chamomile flowers
over the DMT, roll it, lipstick it, almost drag

each out-breath's compassion. As usual, anguish won't know
when it's a crying out from whale places
and when a further might.

Souls of trust will be flayed.
On the freeway, he'll imagine he's a con artist, conning an old woman.
He won't accept what he's having her give him.

MORAVIAN ECLIPSE MYTH

Seven women roam a caldera in the mountains.
One starred in a '90s sketch comedy—wigged
damsel Fabio strummed the lute for. One knows
how arms at sea say, *Save me*, above the waves
and below; her red one-piece's cut grooves
her legs like the grooves in a unicorn's horns.
One is a magician's assistant. One is Ace
Ventura's girlfriend. Two are sisters on *Full House*.
One, an actress who served in my school canteen,
stands a head taller than the rest, neck choke
-chained gold. Down on the flatlands, a villager
gleans the scent. He climbs, and looks. The formation
resembles a deer hoof. I'm the leg. I maneuver
the hoof to a lakeshore, swim it to an island castle.

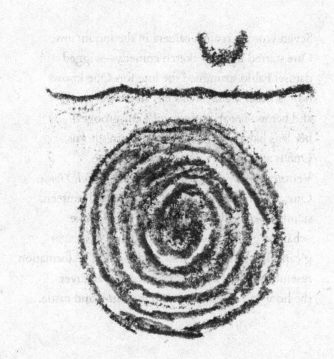

The villager swims the lake. Enters the castle.
His body hair drains. He can't feel his bruises
swell, yellow, but it happens. The bruises are lust
in the way that skin is lust. Hunger too. The bruises
are what his famished village has made of him,
a wandering wound, a balm seeker. Tennis balls
in the guttering when as a boy I'd scale the roof
to retrieve them, felt rain-flayed and soiled to
rags: this is his indigence dress in the darkness
of the great hall. There is one light source—
a mirror, backlit as if with moonlight. Wedged
behind, edging from the bottom, is a scroll.
A kingdom and more for he who slays the ghost
that cannot be slain, whose terror hour is midnight.

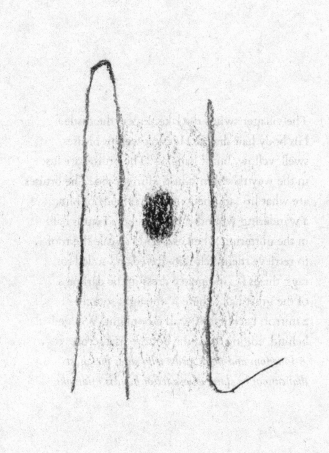

...that cannot be slain, whose terror hour is midnight.
Were the villager literate, he would have read
this, run. But the myth doesn't vest him such power,
nor does a negotiable summons thrill out my chest
hair by the root. He climbs again, up to a garret.
Lights the table candle. Everywhere, the grace of recent
movement: tomes on werewolves, frogs, and dragons
lie open as if just perused, tassels chewed, stroked;
the candle wax is soft and skin-warm; cobwebs
stream off a globe of Earth; shadow cobwebs stream
off the globe's shadow. Between a unicorn's eyes
streams a lone hair, long as a boy is tall—omniscience
and invulnerability in war to whoever plucks it.
Then, the door, wrought of water, not iron, bursts.

Wrought of water, not iron, the garret door bursts.
On the threshold stands a Cyclops. The villager
sees, in that yawning singularity, a servant's quarters
or carriage house in which the captives huddle. *Come!*
Come! It may be a bedroom. Are there bite marks
in the bunk wood? Is Mars' light jaundiced on the ceiling?
It may be a bathroom. Are there razor sheaths
stuck in the heating vent, like truths between teeth?
Nail lines in the grout mould, toy-sniper-green?
The Cyclops attacks. The villager spears its pupil
with the table candle, and from that tumult of sun
-beams and roars carves two perfect halves, which fall.
Out of the split drifts a voice: the damsel. *Kiss the gold*
to claim the gold. The women envelop the villager.

The women envelop the villager. The women
whirled Earth and its shadow. The women, who
were hidden, flare—solar flares. The villager
shields his eyes. The women laugh and bleat and bawl.
In front of the villager sways the actress.
The villager kisses her choker: lips, tongue, teeth.
Her swoon upraises purple smoke, and antlers.
As the smoke settles, seven deer emerge. The deer
bolt the garret. Rather than bask in the blazing
corona that will save his crops, feed him, the villager
dons hunting camouflage. The camo pattern
matches his bruises, as if by design. The masking—
a balm. Need supplants wound—a need I need to hunt.
There is no point, no time. Seven caldera deer run.

THIRD CONTACT

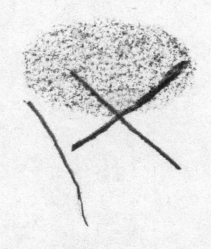

Tunnels

somewhere   between breaths
tunnels open   his tongue
the trowel   that rounds them
tunnels   to lakes
inside   blisters

                   capsicums
inside capsicum   wombs
drink-tap   pupils cold
uterine   headwaters

inside screw   head blackness
inside tree   hollows inside
the *nespola*   tree's poems
of bat   and galah shit

    (declare himself lost more eagerly than other children.) (taste blood
    when he runs for his life.) (report no fears. no allergies, no beloved teachers.)
    decide that to notice is to beg.) (climb out his window cupping his balls
    inside a morning of hot water decanted onto windscreens from milk bottles,
    exhaust fumes thick as flour and water, paperboys skywriting
    with their mouths, the taste of plastic in the frost
    on the plastic the papers lie whole inside like roulade.) (Beg it all.)

inside butterfly   strips that lock
his forehead   blood inside
happiness
no one could feel

                   who hasn't
watched god   descend
from the clouds

                   to cry on paddocks

near dead   from thirst
like he did   on that drive

to   mooloolaba

tunnels   to kimberley
does he   have a crush
kimberley   he always answers
unsmiling
unembarrassed
             practiced
terse

Anaheim, 1997

Cranes beyond the hotel fence—
California Adventure half built.

Disneyland corndogs on the breeze,
batter glint down his t-shirt.

Earlier in the studio tour, he nagged
the guide for a term to capture

the blindness when a black screen
flashed to white like a temper—hot-

air-balloon dawn, the sun's petals
cold in their brazier. The best the guide

could do was film splicers—editing.
His brother *Chinese-burned* his neck.

Now, on the balcony, the Wonder
Woman's uppercut button has broken

and he keeps pressing it, beaten
for height by the top baluster rail,

runners wedged between balusters
for the awe of feeling stuck—no strike.

At their tips, above where Star-Spangled
Banners fly from colossal hooks

the cranes glow, like screens. Mirrors.
Day's terminal shanks. Behind him

through the insect mesh, his dad
lies weeping on his side on the ash

-burnt carpet strip between beds
and TV, Bible facedown, volume dim.

Greensborough Plaza

His mother has to pop into Coles for bread, Panadol, and apples.
She sits him, with some coins from her purse, on a bench by aisle one,
beside a plastic guide dog. Take it off—she tries to fight the dust
mask over his head. The elastic recoils, snares hair, fingers. She blushes,
her eyes dart. She pulls a red basket from the stack. Back on his mouth

and nose, it's damper: his breaths, princesses in the ice-cave
weave that air, butcher-sweet, has kissed. The cold metal nosepiece
shudders him. The Labrador gets one coin. The rest, smelling Donut
King, he pockets, along with coins he stole. In his pockets the number
of UHT milk spout ends hasn't dropped, though he spilled them blaring

up the level ramp. His shoes aren't laced under-over. Unlace totally. Redo.
A pair of old men sit down. Question him. His answers spoon them
life—the Dreamworld log flume ride he's never ridden; litters of pups
his Labrador didn't birth because he has no Lab, no dog; he wears
the mask for allergies; his dad was born in Italy, *ciao, uno, due, tre, quattro*.

While he speaks, he tugs his school shorts, left leg wide as the men's
pant legs, eyelid-tight, slack, irreparable. The men hear his plot to steal
every nosepiece from every dust mask in the Watsonia Mitre Ten for armour
against baddies. The two free donuts his large thickshake comes with
plop into oil, conveyor-belt down to a cinnamon-sugar bath. He's

in a bath, held under. Elation's sharps prick him. Each bite he dunks
in vanilla, guards in his mouth, behind the mask—a freed tooth, too
treasured to swallow. She's bought more than she said. Fizzers—cream
soda—for him. He knows what he must surrender. A deal he made was if
she saw his laces, he'd hug her hips, tell her he loved her, and mean it.

Rules on the Run

Follow the camphor-white cloud
        west past the chick hatchery
RSPCA delicenced, towards Port Phillip,
        offshore. To shiver is to paint
stripes on a squid jig. The seed
        pods trampled into hail slush open
                  portals to the open, to the end
of the line, to salmon-flesh
        -coloured flowers milling
to paste in a pool filter
        bulking the flap door ajar
while on the top step the shallows wince
        while contrast dye floods
                  the neighbours' cat's cranium
(a king brown left it
        other—a sudden, cold birder)
while the cat's third eyelids guillotine
        while cockatoos pull sky's bathplug and wrong has vaulted
while she brings her plants with her
        into the shower perlite dams to the heel
                mantel pot rings laugh aphids
while offshore a squall blows
        apart every squall-gauging instrument
save those not yet built
        while a squid that can't phrase
what threatens it, or what incubates it
        or why it relaxes at free thought
                and action phrased as fealty
plumes white ink that leaches
        to chlorine lightning before it's ever ink
pre-   pre-   pre-
        before the squid no longer pulses

so near the rumpus-room window
            the glass wants every blowfish counted,
every mouth nailed to a face.

Archer

before key
halves for lock

before handle lets go

before gate jump
gills uniform and nylex
asks for tender re-coiling

before marion jones
round side into terrace
with aquarium   back door

before they're
before you   Archer

compound bow
drawn at eighty
cams locked broadhead aquiver like old axolotl
tank

of almost-frogs
to be loosed through yard at
pink boogie board

j-hooked to
punctured trellis

Intervals

Say, *Embraced. Watered. Coffin*
bomb. Playing dead. Playing luge.
There is no afternoon.

Mirror, mirror, how beautiful
I am. The most beautiful man
someone claims they've seen

outside the movies, flattery
that fails to get me in bed, but does
get me in front of a camera

to shoot for the lucrative modelling trial
you tell me the faculty's arranged
with a Toorak Road agency.

Intervals of Pierre Cardin
on the waistband of the little
white briefs I can take home, of prone

and supine, of shutter, of seafloor
where volcano roots. I spring off, grab
handfuls of doghair and lint,

epaulette my slick shoulders,
almost pompous the horse
-power with which I thrust

up the next incline level.
Buy the beautiful man honey
chicken at the casino food court.

Buy him pistachio gelati.
Whisk him to a three-star hotel
with seashells glued to the cistern.

Sleep on a single bed next to his.
Say it's a prize, on the faculty.
Lavish him. He'll let you.

Spirit

Halving olive-oil soap with a cleaver, she says
have your glamour, saint. Vanish. Again
the hangar opens. Really it's a ruined
mental asylum, smokestack-redbrick, deep

in Plenty Gorge bush, where we shot bong
water from our eyes and pus from our nipples and blew
up empties against a mural of bunnies, gophers,
squirrels—eyes night-shade-dipped, arms

daisy-chained, sun laughing, in pastel meadows.
And where we crowbarred rotten plywood
off the cafeteria door, a crow shot out
and Alex shat a little bit. Wrecked a rainbow

lorikeet with slingshot glass. And where
paddy wagons chased us through the pony club
and horse paddocks, one petrified horse
bucked and shat at the same time, its fat dumps

blasting a good fifteen metres into the late-spring
blue, napalming, us laughing like spastics, a red
-haired kid we called Monkey and let hang
around us to fuck with him got his backpack caught

on barbed wire and got done and was lucky
he didn't rat. How many gag on the first shot
of the spirit in the hangar still, but not the second?
And where, behind soggy pink batts and bathroom

cabinets nicked from construction sites, our girls
sucked our cocks—not mine, but I'd pretend
if our girls glanced at me to be on the phone
to someone whose mouth was worthy. Really

it's a padded room, white like white jellybeans, come,
white boys' hairy hamstrings, hagiography, coming
of age in a new-with-tags millennium.
Really it's the quilted jacket I'm wearing.

Map to Mutable Manhood

...no, no, this is too much,
we can not escape to a new continent;
the middle door is judgement...
—H.D., 'Red Rose and a Beggar'

...it will be thousands of years too late.
—Kaveh Akbar, 'Against Hell'

Shred an old atlas into the pit, the last morsel of tinder
you can scrounge in Tom's house
that might save the backyard fire. Consider the smoke
signals heeded. Once his party's over
you're chopper blades on that mattress in the parlour
you always shotgun—storm-scented
but not wet, tags in every language, warped fleurs-de-lis
through the corduroy in gold.
Find his sister's friend's face with your hands. Callused
gondola rides along its canals,
skin so pale it's a light source, like her innocence, her
scout trundle bed's chrome frame.
Hold her face as you would anyone's face but your own.
Hold a sprouted avocado seed.
Hold vanilla gelati, coneless, frozen too solid to weep
down your arms to the crooks.
It's breathless, like a staring contest—you and a boar
dog, a male in hunt armour.
Hold low, valley cloud. You'd have dressed yourself in it
if only it weren't this sheer. Hold
all men against her soft jaw. Her eyes: paintbrush ferrules.
You're twenty, she's seventeen,
you don't want each other, slug tracks enchant the carpet.
I would never hurt you—say it
with your fingers. A boy hurt me, therefore I'm like you,
and like protects like. Don't say it

83

aloud. Tom might stir, ask what the fuck you're doing.
And you'd answer: falling asleep
at a table at the Fairfield boathouse, gums white with
baking soda from the scones.
Sleep as, cream in the webbing of her thoughts, M
unwraps the pink Filofax, earnest
in her thanks, though she's been hinting at pendants.
You're not like the others
—nice as well as handsome, a band saw doubling
as a heat pack stuffed with grain.
You waken for her praise, scoff her leftovers, shout
her a spider, origami her napkins
into a paper plane that flies backwards. Drift off again.
Dream of staring into his soul,
the boar dog. Hold, hold, loving, baleful. Bare your
gaze canines. Next morning
sunlight bangs on the corrugated roof of the shed
you crash in when at Woolamai—
bangs like a drum of boiling sesame-snap caramel.
Hayfevered by the couch dust
you play can-I-hit-the-dartboard-while-sneezing
and lose. Metal nibs on metal
summon the laughter of your mates getting home
from a night with the fat local girl
they tell you they all fucked and blew all over—F
was going at her, then G joined,
then it was open slather. Two more blew in her arse,
one in her hair, which you recall
has flyaways and is long and a complex natural red.
Congratulate them—legends
whose names will live on in songs of their exploits.
Songs sung on 4-chan forums,
honed by belt-buckle bells to a single, universal note.
Songs fathers won't sing to sons
until they're ready. Epics, anthems, manifestos, prayers.
Rebuke yourself for not going.

You're a pussy. A weak faggot, like the joke. Fuck you
and the jetty squids you watched
once the others had left for the house down the road,
the squids you told secrets.
You're trying to silicone-seal the wind that's turned
a strait between you cyclonic,
vaster than an almond orchard, narrower than a fine
girl's waist when she's bending it.
The surf is a mess. Waves suck out hunks of shore
sand like kite talons through rabbit.
It's impossible to float on your back and sky-dream
with your body-board flailing
on its leash like that—Velcro-burned wrists, salt
-burned throat, balls, lungs, eyes.
Leap into those beetle bushes. French-kiss letterboxes
with a cricket bat, with the lips
of a pipe wrench, down Zigzag Road at rum speed.
At one house, a brindled dog
jumps the gate and tries to jump onto your ute tray,
lead your hunt. Instinct
tells you he's savage. But he's oil, spilled on the road.
A colossal break dumps you
at the entrance to your tent, which has collapsed, or
all but collapsed, in the storm
that wrecked the main stage before Empire of the Sun
(it's 2008—this is everything).
Your air mattress, toenail-lanced, is a carpet. Scattered
across the carpet are five-dollar
notes, all fives, like pink detention slips—also a NSW
license she won't see again. Read
the scatter pattern. What's it say? Read it like a man.
The part where you abstain
from handing the license in, press it eyes-up in the mud.
Read the fish-and-chip menu,
buy three family packs with tartare sauce, pineapple
fritters, sorry for the small tender.

Read the part where you hold her hip granite as she
tenses above you, slackens, neither
of you enjoys it, and it's as if someone is slapping
bucketfuls of tomato juice
against the tent roof and walls, and someone else has
two leaf blowers, a villain
wielding a pair of swords to slash at the heroes. Both
you and she wear rain gear.
By not trying to unbutton her jeans, you're saying
I don't understand how
to be a sexual man and not an animal—do with me
as much or as little as you want
and that discretion will be my God. You're saying
I'll bite off the almond husks,
I'll scale that crumbling church without a harness,
I'll swim to the farthest buoy,
I'll fist-pump down a black run, I'll fill an anklet
with train rocks, but won't swing,
my impotence is my God in this, in this negation
of negation. I am not
the things a man is not that make him terrifying
—the legend in the songs—
and that, stranger, is completeness. You're saying
where's my sympathy?
I didn't choose for my come to be scooped up
and eaten in another room
while exit shocks messed the bathwater tide. Pity
my band of ciphers—men
hurt by a patriarchy that means they could hurt,
devilled by that potentiality.
Do as I say. And here she is, in your tent, letting
five-dollar notes like blood.
It's breathless, like a tight weave—you and a boar
dog, a male in hunt armour.
Your hand still cold with the front-door brass
admit that boys and girls

can't go to the movies together without fuck lust.
Forget what you saw with Sally
just now. Or how in maths her g-string got loose
that time, the boys screamed
dirtily, blushed, you blushed, but you were quiet.
Such objections are dead,
masochistic. So you submit more facts to the case
against your brother's girlfriend's
right to shit on his honour. In support of the screams.
Portsea. Your longtime friend
sits at a granite kitchen island, watches online rape
accusations thrum in like surf
raised by the chant of watercraft on the Goulburn,
the Murray—surf-proof
except as horsepower imposes it. *To worry* also means
to produce waves in Russian.
Did you know shopping trolley poles can be kicked
loose and brandished as weapons?
Someone at the masculinity talk says so. The keynote
cites evolutionary psychology
that may lead to harmony between the sexes, may
lead to the next incel massacre.
Did you know streetlights can be booted out if you
boot the pole hard enough?
Wiring inside gets jogged, stunned. It goes dark.
But only for a few seconds.
Did you know you can get anal Fleshlights now, exact
molds of pornstars' arses?
Always the Megabus stops at the roadhouse in view
of the sex store, a maroon barn
you're seldom tempted by, before it hits Ann Arbor
and you buy the good organic
tampons for S, who needs two at once for her septate
condition and has changed
names to C, gender to non-binary,
and the songs you sing her, her, her, don't represent

your ability to scale the swollen
almond tree and rattle it for them. Rainmaker, they
value you. If only you could
drop the shameful urge to categorise what's valued
according to your leg hair
which you've spiked with gel for their amusement
or how the yoghurt-and-charcoal
face mask stains your stubble into ghoulish relief.
Or, do the urge and the urge's
criticism combined form a category, the masculine
ironic, if the distance between
intention and action is the distance between cities,
one safe, the other at war?
An unmapped distance. A dam awaiting its perch,
a dog its armour's removal.
Near your parents', there's a farm-to-table restaurant.
You spend over the voucher
to get a better white than the house, warm ginger
snaps on your *tres leches* cakes.
E you regale with the legend of when three nangs
at once didn't fell you.
More blurted, godless things as the wine's presented.
She's openness, she's order,
she's the shock of a breaching fiord dolphin. She's
the bridge of the right hand
your left hand caresses, ready to be lavender, ready
to listen all night.

As It Lies

Grass-sweet air, sweetness
cut with barbecue smoke—
yellow onions blackening.
Ominous pollen count.
The family goes for a drive
to Yan Yean, to the reservoir
they like. Few other families
have had the same thought
and they nab the best rotunda
atop a fresh-mown hill. Best
barbecue (some don't heat
to any degree of use; some
are dirty). The two big sons
play chicken with the father
on his backswing as he drives
golf balls, illegally, downhill.
The mother halves lemons,
degreases the heating barbecue,
discards the blackened
and juiced halves, flat like pucks,
corona of fruit shards at the rim.
Game magpies close in,
scatter, close in, scatter.
Beside the mother, the little son
sucks his thumb and dozes.
Lungs salivate for the sweet
air chilled by catchment water
the sparkling of which looks
to the middle son like his head
when the lights go out—
when inside his head lights up.
Hook, slice, slice—the father

tells the sons he's lost form
since last time. Range balls—
yellow like the daffodil dust
stoking the mother's allergies
—speckle the hillside. Hot
-plate: wing marinade, honey-
soy, seeps under the sausages
like he (the middle son) likes.
That way, the undersides blacken.
That way, I leave out the boy
who will be a cruelty to them,
who can't speak of childhood
without belting them to account,
can't go to bed without bedding
menace, can't love and love
what's right in it. I dare to smear
the family campfire stories
with less marshmallow ash.
Who cares if it's impossible—
to the father in a thistle rough
playing the ball as it lies,
to the mother who nose is red
less from despair than allergies,
to the baby whose spit thumb
robs coldness from the breeze
and whose eyes will grow less
than the parts he'll cut and burn
and whose eyes sparkle with
catchment water, and even to
the oldest son, so charming
and imitable and confused, I
leave an unbruised memory,
a day of sweetness and rest.
The sausages turn out perfect,
the onions black, but not burnt
so that char is all you taste.

With his Christmas Victorinox,
into the gashed picnic-table
face, the oldest son carves his
initials, and those of his brothers.
The father and mother let him.

Crooner

if i am infected
then as you ate and drank me
as you
keyed my height

and i your height
into the canoe outside
the livery   didn't reel

from the boy in rollerblades
who shat on his doorstep

brakes rendering
glitter from concrete

underpants stuffed
behind gas meter

yabby bait meat greying in a dam

neighbours drumming
beers on brick
father hosing   denial

as this song is for you
the song of the crooner in zia's

parlour on christmas
whom elba women whose lyrics
won italy's most salacious

wrapped   a leek's pale core

for whom they drummed mud
hosiery   pleasured mandolins

let you be the crooned
of forest   i the rabbit
let the rabbit who might love you
pass without a pawprint

Valour

an act   an act

everyone witness every moment

witness them
gash their head on the headboard

witness the mouse's heart

caged in their heart   witness the sweet

man   pipe serene
tinctures into guava juice

valorous
manacle
                witness   them ask

why laugh after he told
                who touched him

told who for the first time
and he wasn't laughing

                                                        but a hologram close
                                                            laughter beamed
the free falcon laughs back at the mews

witness in matching black bamboo underwear them hurt themselves him restrain them

valorous   witness him tell who

that it might confer the power
to overpower   witness him as penance

eat the wall

                                                    plaster from their hair

a priesthood of rats   recite their matins

                    you had no right
had no right where thumbnail
                        moons should crest   moonless

FOURTH CONTACT

Puberty

                                        somewhere between
                                        swimming carnival

                                    and midnight bath
                                    a body sees itself

                                eats roe off unibrow
                                roots foothair roots
                            smells come in callery
                            pear blossom

                        behind the toolshed
                        smelts lego breeds

                    its palms scalding
                    skinning

                smells come in a tub
                of starry blue putty
            splits apricot pits
            splits their almonds

        folds back its eyelids
        putties an ocean pisses
    the name girls chanted
    across the border

fence where its house is
and is not its house

The Last Poem

The first liberty is the liberty to say everything.
—Maurice Blanchot, translated by Susan Hanson

Midnight, courtyard lamplit
more day than the day. She
sits opposite him; hounds
-tooth brickwork lends this
the air, the lounge, of high fashion.
Everything's in the open
that should be. Those from
whom parts had to be veiled
sleep in warmth. The few who
had to be devastated have
found disclosure's silhouette
so graceful it's been nothing,
a *felix culpa*. No torched lives.
No vestibule, no holding pattern.
Where aggression has been
pleaded for, the throat has
ennobled it. The Monterey
pine was never pick-axed.
Never wept its spearmint.
Under the blood moon, deer
shadows streak an open field
parallel to train tracks behind her.
Again the blood moon
brings the Cyclops whose eye
seeks the spear, but he doesn't
ask why again. Some choices
aren't forgivable. Those who
should know this do now
and have borne it well. Better than dreamt.
Soft power has triumphed.
Lamplight razes blemish

from their skin, siliconises it, dolls
it. Laughter has no form
to lodge. Their gazes meet.

Quicklime

And so this flaw within the silk
of memory began to run –
—John A. Scott, Run in the Stocking

Rain boils. A liar
wakes eating the hairs on his hands.

Failure, again, to alarm
the eyes fast enough to shock
unstalked world.

At breakfast, he and his parents
will share a bowl of *nespole* from the tree. They might
reminisce—*nespole* boiling

to jam in glut months. Batsong
will mandate whether they'll know what the fruit
or they know.

World where he arrests himself
behind just fault. A liar goes to piss, the dog
blocks the corridor

near her bed, mid-seizure, moon's
quicklime spilled up her, *nespola*-pit
-pupiled. Froth shellacs jowls, chest.

Compost? King brown? Maybe
the man he saw seizure at the library so ardently
opposed an ambulance

because lightning needn't yoke
to the struck. World where control dreams
like surrender. A liar kisses her belly, it's

alright, my girl. Doubt
wakes the eyes: rip apart; welcome.

Range

there is no boardwalk down to the spit   you improvise arcing
blundstone-prints round the cove as far as the sand will bear you
smearing whitebait on *revegetation zone* pickets in the dunes. tackle
in the box he has let you   tall as mum's clavicle   guard
clatters. he holds the rods   berley   whitebait bag. it sweats it's
fetid. the sun burns your ears   bleaches the down on the lobes.
when you reach a slight headland   you have to embrace it concede
your boots must drown if you're to round it   on a rock-pool
ledge   and reach the spit he reckons is like raiding a trout farm.
they drown. he rigs your new k-mart shimano. baits it. you cast.

parts i cannot propitiate. voices outside the range to transmit the signals

the seashell nonna used as a bookend in her last house   before
she fell. you took turns listening to it. to its white noise   voices
on the outside modulated through it   voices opened up like chests
of voices. one afternoon in the bathroom   its appeal strikes you
seashell filters are semiconscious filters   the filters vertigo
for erosion puts to its ear and listens   world-sound
from the brink. foam at his mouth-edges pops. his thumb and index
sink into your neck's lymph nodes. your eyes meet. a sea binds you.
cartilage embayment   mutual sight's isthmus   irenic absorption
of lure rust into the pores of tackle-box plastic   towel-rack buoy.

the outside voices cannot transmit. i parts range to propitiate the signals.

alternate synthesis: apology pact erasure complaisance return
        flight death sententiousness hatred recompense
        flight return refrain return delusion flight
            flight return vengeance
                flight refrain
                    flight

Face of Glory

bear in   mind
false positives must

be   confirmed
for state   records

by a final   test
my   apologies

              i   chose
to alert   you

friday as   a pre
caution   you

must   have   had
a difficult weekend

Cathedral

Can you think, the doctor asks,
of what might have led to this? *Who
did you fuck and how did you fuck them.*
Stand with me in the snow, on the call.

Observe the hawk in a linden sapling,
massive for the frail limb, an absurdity,
buckling it. Students surround the hawk.
So unlit a morning, they use flash.

Glance over the chapter of the novel
I'm writing when the table vibrates
about twin brothers a woman hurts.
Who did you fuck and how did you fuck them.

It's a mess, I grant you. Self-serving
to apply to the doctor's question that logic
of the novel which abhors vacuums
in causality—to spiral to the beginning, plant

in the linden sapling a hawk
before a millipede. What have a childhood's
given and made to do with the falsehood
or truth of this? Glean in the unlit snow

how they have everything to do with it.
How for years this certitude could build
around it a wound radius, a cathedral
steeped in incense and a knighting

of the order of fated victimhood. Stand
with me in retrospect. I was never at risk.
False positives are as rare as totalities;
less rare for straight, lucky men. Read

the ode to that luck, but don't forget that
day really did look like night, quieted birds, lulled
man to boy—*who did you fuck and how did you fuck them.*
Examine the brave knight's heraldry.

Stand with hawk. Stand with ring-tail.
Stand with hawk, who has pinned
this dualism's privilege by the neck
for judgment. Judge it. Is it redeeming?

Assent

        maybe with it the curdled parts that rise
when some haul their melting

piss glaciers to the laundry   hicky

their own calves   finger-abseil their throat

maybe it won't sour like the milk baby
        them throws up   re-drinks as legend

            has it

out of avarice
        later
axes warping
        later
a bath
horseplay
conspiratorial grins

        maybe rainforest in suburban redbrick

tar pits in boys with lovely parents   actors

at whose toes no bouquets collapse

maybe some wrists that cock to heat the water need

its turning   its earnest turning

        maybe to think of grafting pleasure
to watching some die of thirst is to

think of a planet with days so long you can bolt

get caught   hurt   get free

and the sun's high   childlike

Strawberry Dawn

The current sluices through her toes, rendering them in duck shit.
     She picks at a whitehead on her shoulder.
She wears a bra with solid black straps, sheer cups—expensive.
          He doesn't wear any clothes.
He didn't notice her remove it, but her navel diamante is gone.

They have smoked too much ice. Anyone but them could see that,
     but there isn't anyone else
for kilometres. Everyone is either asleep at camp, or off dancing.
        Overhead: dawn red-gum ashtanga.
Inside the pipe they smoke from, smoke more, it's bituminous.

As she swims, she tongues the gap between her teeth—bloodshot
     contortionist urging herself
through an enamel frame. Green mud daubs her emergent
       belly. The deadwood outcrop slime
grants her fingers no purchase, feet no traction, so he pulls her up.

They get to be kissing, the sun gets itself ascended, influential. She
       tastes of chemicals and river water.
In vain they try to fuck in the water. This is the third morning in a row
that they have not wakened. This has nothing at all to do with it.

He mentions the cat and axolotl cemetery, beneath the Monterey
     pine in his childhood backyard. He plays
dumb when she asks him was he at ejaculation
       age for his first orgasm. That supple
rime the axolotls got, white shadow, before death; he mentions it

and laughs. Deep down, they're drawn to each other for the hyper
  -commiseration, the overtasked body.
At different times their heads return to the home key after vagrant
              harmonic wandering. Strawberries
ripen on blue vines. They smoke more. The Murray parents them.

Silences

*Conocsco una città
che ogni giorno s'empie di sole
e tutto è rapito in quel momento*
—*Giuseppe Ungaretti, 'Silenzio'*

1

He DJ's a friend's Italian-themed party.
There's getting into the spirit
and getting into the spirit: they've
papier-mâchéd lion heads over the newel posts,
bought two three-litre Aperols.

2

when the discman no longer.   cold-burns his chest

no longer not chest.   stars   no longer doored teeth

when the bicarb soda dunes atop his bookshelf   are cadence

3

You need a green armband and to be under twelve
to play on the inflatable pontoon race circuit
in the daylight hours. Captain's armbands—
in the daylight hours, every child is captain of this river,
bodies so light as not to disturb the trapped air.

4

pedestrian tunnel
years of overlaid graffiti
cobalt sea / caution tape
years of cobwebbed
cages around the lights
freed morning
amber to bolt through
scorpion in amber my name
the maiden vessel

5

of cleaning mess
                    of mess not yet cleaned

of mess not noticed
                    of noticed mess left

6

　　　　　such as when providence is
　　　　　the drain grating he slips on
　　　　　jeans and knees asphalt-opened
　　　　　close enough to smell the Brut
　　　　　of the gatecrasher he was leading
　　　　　the hunt up the driveway for—the gatecrasher
　　　　　pain drowns out the pack escorting
　　　　　to surgery, jaw and eye sockets
　　　　　slurried, braces through gums, lips.

7

blood cyclone in his ears
morning orchids
lamp beads

1

Big cardboard Roman columns, flags,
Davids. One housemate has wedged
an extra 50mg, free of charge,
into each MDMA capsule—
gold-class shit, direct from bikies.

8

                    brother's over
                    time at the mush
                    room factory

3

White boardshorts lambent in the dark
he dog-paddles to the pontoon. Cottonwood
seed fluff spurs the river, as though millions

of teddy bears have been slit open
and scattered in the water as burley. Some he eats,
washes down with water that tastes of loam and wool.

Moonlight lets him study the complex
ideograms along the pontoon's side. No
diving, they seem to command, but what's the difference

between diving and bound-to-happen falling?
These curved lines—they must
describe passage underneath.

9

when in a dream her voice.   bluff collapses onto the quarantine station
eden's white room   when there's no.   waking   movement

my body   bitter   shark

bitter.   at being up all
night

by itself   circling   in carnage it wrecks itself
to secrete   bitter that sleep   won't dragnet it

8

Take a small carrot from the crisper
to the bathroom where he takes orchids
you'll smell for the rest of your life,
feel on your fingers like an imminence
of resin. Coat the carrot in face moisturiser,
your mother's expensive rosehip one.
Insert it. Prance to the lounge room.
Someone could come home any minute blankets
could gag you any minute. Strain your torso
to hear the huntsman's trail from earlier, when you left
the pool, and on the ping-pong table a towel
lay crumpled and a nest. The huntsman
in the screen-door glass you saw coming up you
along a trail you strain to hear now, for nothing
else than to hear how those screams sounded
not like your voice, but a girl's, like the boy
at the bus stop whose hair you set ablaze, as if real
fear forgot its finishing. In soapy water

sterilise the carrot. Put it back, paper-towel-
wisped. Unknow it. Count aloud, baritone,
how long before the fridge motor quiets.

10

Morning orchids
sky urn
tisane

1

He plays recklessly, mixes well. Loops,
for example, the beginning of Franchi's *Cream*,
bringing it up so slowly people aren't sure
he's bringing it up, until he cuts the loop and the synth opens, and thirty
-year-olds are nineteen for a few minutes.

The dance-floor's dark—an aromatherapy
steam room, but with Lamborghini cologne.
To see the mixer, he shines his phone flashlight
as his brother shone a Maglite on him in his bunk
and said, Andy, I'm a stuntman in an action movie.

Lowering his head over the mixer is water
rumbling through a weir into backwaters.
Fondness for the set takes ketamine form.
Thirty minutes into the ninety, his one miscue
is to venture a piece of spacious Italian

techno that migrates focus inwards, body to spirit,
myth to bildungsroman, propane heater
sucking oxygen from a dark caravan. He can see
eyes lid. Hands pity their opposite wrists.
Greed: to ask them to stay.
He backspins the jog wheel as if it were real vinyl, cues Madison Avenue.

One mate keeps gushing about his shirt: black silk,
gold / red / green filigree, gold Versace-esque lions.
It's this mate's dream shirt. Look at him—DJ,
living the dream. Off his back he swaps the shirt
for three MDMA caps, haggled to two.

3

Monkey bars, abacus, rope climb.
All flawless: give him a captain's armband
even if adult triceps are pythons

and adult wrists claustrophobic.
Half yabby, half rock, the captain dives
to the colder membrane, more mud than water,
near the bed. Deep enough to ascend
with his arms raised above him, fingers
raised, so that at first contact

with the quilted, algae-slimed PVC
he bounces off—a rocket over
-eager to dock to the mothership.

11

such as when his body gives itself back to him
and he pities it and is a vengeful god towards it
that it would be so giving. such as when, before anyone
is awake (his mother has been death-dreaming
every night and may be awake) he turns on the shower
in his and his brother's bathroom. notices, as the water heats,
dried blood on the shag mat and tiles. the little
bin heaped with blood tissues. such as when the tiles
shudder his knees. when he folds the mat
as he would a love letter to be shepherded
around a classroom, as if iodine and clothes-peg
rust were code for he wants to suck you. such as when
he lays the parcel in the laundry basket, pats it,
a pastry cook knocking air from sweet dough,
empties the little bin into the big outside bin,
scrapes off the tile blood with the scouring side of a sponge,
drops the sponge into the big outside bin, finds
the linen closet's whitest mat, lays it neat, lays it
square, and there's no trace of the shower's readiness.

1

Someone he hardly knows tells him an uncle in the cult touched her.
They're in an alley, after his set. Dew has happened.
He tells her he was—not by whom. They embrace.
Do drugs. Later, he waits inside near the front door for his Uber,
a traitor to his queens, stabbing teeth with his tongue.

12

Morning orchids
uterine

3

Above the entrance to Dubrovnik's Old City
Saint Blaise carries the city in miniature.

On the garage roof above a pool lit squid–blood
blue in the night, a boy hears past impacts fizz.

The pontoon does not hear its carrier
—discarnate, infinite.

1

Disturbance in the front bedroom.
Uber delayed, he goes in. A few mates
at the bedside, including the guy in his shirt
drip water from their fingers
onto the lips of a blonde girl

who's blown out on G and will not
be alive in a few months. She accepts
some of the droplets into her mouth,
deflates onto her side towards a chain
of paper Italian flags on the wall.

As a parting gift, he's given a column
and a David, like novelty cheques.
Ears ringing, numb with cold, he walks up the cul de sac
towards the car on his phone screen.
Morning orchids.

13

of that.
that waits

Ars Poetica

Who gets to play *mercy* with himself—figure-four leglock, Ventolin
-scar, and monumentalise himself. Whose cells each steal an aorta.
Who gets to taste that the Agassi-Sampras semi-final has a word.
Who, from a tennis racquet's throat he cracks, digs out power cells
of graphite, rubs them between his fingers until they're within him.
A girl at school gets detention and a sorry for saying God ravished her.
From hot public water, initiates emerge robed in one another's skin.
Another carat of tissue, another licence to tell someone listening.
Who gets to tell or not tell. Whose not telling is a telling. A form.
Whose nonna says, *Se non fosse per la grazia divina, quello sarei io*: there for it
go they. Decades after Hiroshima, some survivors believe they're still carriers
of death; doctors label them prophets, magic, for this contagion. Who gets
a full summit. Whose name is a magic word, turning *trauma* to *trailhead*.
Witness in German: *zeugen*—also *procreate*. Who gets to commit such
joy will carry his offspring full-term, will round his bellies of wonder.

Palm Cove

Three nights they heard the curlew cry.
It is the warning known of old
That tells them one tonight shall die.
—Kath Walker, 'The Curlew Cried'

Beach cleared: saltwater sighting.
On his zia's balcony, she reads
about the Vedas—their dawn ardour.

He learns local flying-fox colonies
have been cooking to death, and how

as a child, his favourite poet
hammered rocks
against rocks in the hinterland
near school, every spark

a vow. At night, they adore each other as they have many times.
Geckos on cyclone shutters witness. As they have many times

they feel a child between them,
tropic-warm, submitting.

She soothes the child. With tenderness
says she's never meant more to him
than an old escape to pull off.

She doesn't hear his koans on agency or cleft touch.
How could she?

The bush stone-curlews have begun.
A fugue, holding them
until whitecaps catch.

Intervals

Limestone unmasks as keys.
Tunnel into freezer, burn
the deed to breath, redraft it.

Mountain incline, standing pedal.
Intervals of handlebar and X,
volcano and the craters

where biceps meet forearms,
where a decade of eclipse meets
accounts of swimsuit pageants

schoolboys in Perth, Adelaide, New Zealand, Durham, grown
boys now, prayed they'd win—
win praise. Where pure wool

suit meets prison scrubs, doghair.
Where cowlicked forehead
almost hang-glides the gulf

between hotel beds, narrowed
at intervals, like sculpture; almost
lets a cop's big grip from behind

spare it the car door jamb. Intervals
of thrash and limpness, of silk
-worm and silk. Of sugar trucks, America.

Admit I had you choose me. Master
key. Admit it was random.
Admit my final pose struck fear.

Summit—pre-descent bells.
Intervals of lint, of owed might, of the vain
scan for fury, of afternoon.

Say, *This is here. This is the future*
border I shut and opened in real
loving intervals. Blur. Panorama.

Daylesford Fire Bath

Dad reaches into the pool-filter
fuse box. Takes smoking flight, tremors
the bricks at my feet, a beggar

before a king—eels in his lips
say, *Forgive me*, too formal, not my father
but the man who nearly took him.

This man sweats my response, neither of us wise
to how corrupt it already is,
like you and I wait for sun to sanction
our hair masques while corellas

puncture bath steam, pageant gully.
No supplicant. No sovereign. No coins
in the bag of magnesium salt

you're emptying. No weight
to tare, only moss that absolves water, love's
revolutions—and yes,

that's all too cryptic. We write the densest
code to firewall ourselves

from ourselves. Corrode people, like thirst. Spare them
by being dead to them—you get the gist. You know

I still wonder if being violated
made me a better person. A gentler man.

You know *ladder*, *aerial* were my first words—
the first I have orders to revolt and claim
forgiveness spoke.

That any of this should be radical.
Name. Answer. Dusk. Bombs of colour
effervescing from hand to hand.

For Emily

Baily's Beads

Y photographs X
after they've fucked, sunk into siesta
slick and dreamless as stones
in a white flax dam, risen. *You're pretty.*
    Wear them.

Afternoon in grade five
Teacher Polaroids X for the classroom wall
says as the shutter clicks *You*
are so good-looking, and a grown-up says *I*
    am, aren't I?

Pretty like Baily's Beads
when moon meets sun, loves sun
or ruins sun (the myths vary), and lunar
mountains are jewels, lunar
    valleys jewels.

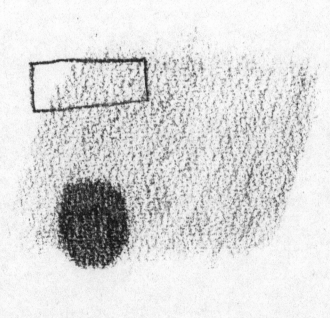

Oracle Bones

Day *xin-si*. There was a *rhi zi* in the western sky.
Will it bring disaster?
(diviner / asker / verification lost)

August 13. A short-lived malady
lives on in shadows. Are they permanent?
Not with sacrifice.

Day *gui-wei*. Divination performed by Zheng.
Will there be no disaster
in the next ten days?
(asker / verification lost)

June 18. The crack forms portended
he would always be a scourge to lovers.
July 06. It was put forth
that birch and cypress sprigs be offered.

Day *gui-you*. The Sun was eclipsed in the evening; is it good?
The Sun was eclipsed in the evening; is it bad?
(diviner / asker / verification lost)

September 09. He asked if he could forgive.
(verification lost)

From day *yi-mao* to the next was foggy. Three flames
ate the Sun, and there were big stars.
(diviner / asker / question lost)

Note

'Oracle Bones' quotes from 'Astronomy on Oracle Bone Inscriptions' by Xu Zhen-tao, F.R. Stephenson, and Jiang Yao-tiao. *Quarterly Journal of the Royal Astronomical Society*, vol. 36, 1995, pp.397–406.

Acknowledgements

I wish to acknowledge the traditional owners of the lands on which much of this book was written: Ann Arbor, Michigan; Chicago, Illinois; and northeastern Melbourne, Australia. I pay my respects to elders past, present, and emerging.

I am grateful to the editors of the following publications in which poems from *Totality* appeared, sometimes in earlier versions: *Australian Book Review* 430; *Australian Poetry Anthology* 2018 and 2019; *Cordite Poetry Review* 87; *Overland* 232 and 236; *Plenitude* January 2021 (Canada); *PRISM* 58.2 (Canada); *Rabbit* 30; *Sick Leave Journal* 'Naughty'; *Westerly* 65.2. 'Pedagogy' was longlisted for *PRISM*'s 2020 Pacific Spirit Poetry Prize.

Heartfelt thanks to Shane and the Recent Work Press team for believing in this project at a time when opportunities to publish poetry collections are scarce.

My PhD supervisor, John Hawke, was an invaluable first reader—and editor—of many of these poems. I also received vital feedback from Eva Birch.

I would not have been capable of attempting this book, let alone completing it, without the friends, family, and professionals who gave me, who give me, the one gift that matters: trusting, compassionate recognition.

Alis, my grandmother, died before I published my first poem. Not long ago, I learned that she wrote poetry in her youth, and even won awards. What I would give to recover those poems; they'd be reason enough to learn Italian. I dedicate this book to Nonna and the kinship she and I share, a century apart.

Emily. Thank you, *carina*.

About the Author

Anders Villani holds an MFA from the University of Michigan's Helen Zell Writers' Program, where he received the Delbanco Prize for poetry. His first collection, *Aril Wire,* was released in 2018 by Five Islands Press. Anders's poetry has appeared in many local and international publications, including *Overland, Southerly, Westerly, PRISM International* (Canada), and *Two Cities Review* (USA). PhD candidate at Monash University, assistant poetry editor of *Australian Book Review*, and an ABR Rising Star, he lives in Melbourne.

About the Artist

Tyler Arnold lives and works on Gadigal land, Sydney. He recently completed a two year residence at the Dunmoochin Foundation, which he used to hone his oil painting practice of landscape and portrait painting. He works across painting, drawing, performance and music. Tyler's work was Commended in the Naked & Nude Art Prize in 2021 and he was awarded the Norma Bull Portraiture Scholarship in 2019 in both cases for life size self portraits.

www.ingramcontent.com/pod-product-compliance
Ingram Content Group Australia Pty Ltd
76 Discovery Rd, Dandenong South VIC 3175, AU
AUHW020721050325
407891AU00005B/39